W9-BFE-239

Social Media's Star Power:

The New Celebrities and Influencers

Social Media's Star Power:

The New Celebrities and Influencers

Stuart A. Kallen

ReferencePoint
Press

San Diego, CA

© 2021 ReferencePoint Press, Inc.
Printed in the United States

For more information, contact:
ReferencePoint Press, Inc.
PO Box 27779
San Diego, CA 92198
www.ReferencePointPress.com

ALL RIGHTS RESERVED.
No part of this work covered by the copyright hereon may be reproduced or used in any form or by any means—graphic, electronic, or mechanical, including photocopying, recording, taping, web distribution, or information storage retrieval systems—without the written permission of the publisher.

LIBRARY OF CONGRESS CATALOGING-IN-PUBLICATION DATA

Names: Kallen, Stuart A., 1955- author.
Title: Social media's star power : the new celebrities and influencers / by Stuart A. Kallen.
Description: San Diego, CA : ReferencePoint Press, [2021] | Includes
    bibliographical references and index.
Identifiers: LCCN 2020012340 (print) | LCCN 2020012341 (ebook) | ISBN
    9781682829318 (library binding) | ISBN 9781682829325 (ebook)
Subjects: LCSH: Social media--Juvenile literature. | Internet
    personalities--Juvenile literature. | Social influence--Juvenile literature.
Classification: LCC HM742 .K35 2021 (print) | LCC HM742 (ebook) | DDC
    302.23/1--dc23
LC record available at https://lccn.loc.gov/2020012340
LC ebook record available at https://lccn.loc.gov/2020012341

Contents

The New Entertainment

In 2007 two brothers from Birmingham, Alabama, began posting video blogs on their YouTube channel. Hank and John Green, now known as the Vlogbrothers, conversed with one another, sang songs, and promoted their favorite charities, education, and general "nerd" culture. The Vlogbrothers rapidly built an audience of dedicated fans called Nerdfighters who support the Greens' championing of intellect and the "fight" against mediocrity. By 2010 the Nerdfighter community had grown so large that the Green brothers decided to launch an annual three-day conference. VidCon would be a place where the online video community could gather, swap ideas, perform, and party.

Around fourteen hundred people attended the first VidCon, held in a hotel basement in Los Angeles. The following year attendance nearly doubled to twenty-five hundred, and in 2012 the conference attracted more than seven thousand to the Anaheim Convention Center. Interest in VidCon continued to grow as more and more people dreamed of becoming social media celebrities like the Greens. By 2015 VidCon was attracting more than hopeful YouTubers. Major corporate sponsors such as Calvin Klein, Samsung, and Hasbro were there looking for influencers to promote their products. Hollywood movie studios like 20th Century Fox, Universal Pictures, and Warner Bros. used the event to connect with video creator culture while trying to build excitement among the influential, young audience for upcoming films.

In 2019 over thirty thousand people paid from $100 to $600 to attend VidCon. Journalist Julia Alexander describes the scene: "YouTube creators loomed over the convention as royalty; they stared down at young, obsessive fans from massive posters hanging from the convention building, and walked around flanked by security guards, passing through secret passageways to their destinations."[1] The scene was similar at the VidCons held in England, Australia, and Singapore that year. On the tenth anniversary of VidCon in 2020, two more events were scheduled, in Mexico and the United Arab Emirates. By this time VidCon events were attracting nearly one hundred thousand people who were focusing on building their social media star power.

VidCon is an annual conference where members of the online video community can gather to swap ideas, perform, and party.

Building Digital Chatter

The job of social media star barely existed in 2010. Today it is seen as one of the most desirable jobs. A 2019 Harris poll of three thousand children ages eight through twelve found that a majority of kids hoped to become YouTubers or vloggers one day. And YouTuber beat former top desirable occupations like teacher, astronaut, musician, and professional athlete. As YouTuber DeStorm Power comments, "Every time I go to schools, the most said thing from 90% of kids is, 'I want to be a YouTuber.' They want to be social-media stars."[2]

Social media stars might be called TikTokers, the Instafamous, the Twitterati, or YouTubers, depending on their favorite platforms.

> "Every time I go to schools, the most said thing from 90% of kids is, 'I want to be a YouTuber.'"[2]
>
> —DeStorm Power, YouTube star

Whatever they are called, social media stars attract attention by creating vlogs, blogs, gamecasts, tutorials, and other videos. Almost all of the internet famous use their social media fame to earn money as influencers. They promote consumer goods to influence the purchasing decisions of their fans and followers. These promotions build what marketers call digital chatter—that is, people talking about their products online. And as the corporate presence at VidCon shows, this chatter is extremely valuable; according to *Ad Age*, businesses are expected to spend $15 billion on influencer marketing by 2022.

The explosive growth of wannabe social media stars and influencers follows a massive shift away from traditional media sources like television and movies. The popularity of video-on-demand services is exploding, and young people have learned to filter out conventional advertising and commercials, online and off. With a shrinking number of TV watchers, advertisers are desperate to reach postmillennials. These people, aged sixteen to twenty-two, often referred to as Gen Z, are glued to their phones. A large majority spend more than four hours a day on TikTok, Instagram, YouTube, and other online sites watching videos and following their favorite social media stars.

Here to Stay

A 2019 poll by Morning Consult found that a whopping 54 percent of Americans aged thirteen to thirty-eight would become a social media influencer, given the chance. And anyone with a video camera, an internet connection, and a willingness to work hard and build an audience can become an influencer. But for every successful YouTuber there are thousands who have failed—less than four out of every one hundred videos posted on YouTube will make money. And very few hopefuls become as famous as vlogger Zach King, with 21 million followers, or beauty expert Huda Kattan, with 29 million followers.

While the likelihood of achieving success as a social media star is minuscule, influencer culture is a well-established force that is playing a growing role in society. Journalist Kevin Roose writes, "It's increasingly obvious to me that the teenagers and 20-somethings who have mastered these platforms—and who are often dismissed as shallow, preening narcissists by adults who don't know any better—are going to dominate not just internet culture or the entertainment industry but society as a whole."[3] As Roose makes clear, the influencer culture of today is molding the visionaries of entertainment and marketing of the future. Those who can steer the online conversation will find success in whatever field they choose, be it media, politics, or business.

> "The teenagers and 20-somethings who have mastered [social media] platforms. . . . are going to dominate not just internet culture or the entertainment industry but society as a whole."[3]
>
> —Kevin Roose, journalist

Chapter One

Billions of Hits, Millions of Dollars

After her photos were posted to Reddit in 2012, she became an instant internet celebrity. By 2019 she had 8.2 million followers on Facebook and an additional 2.7 million on Instagram and 1.5 million on Twitter. Her You-Tube channel had 282,000 subscribers, and her internet fame brought attention from the mainstream media. She appeared on *American Idol*, *The Bachelorette*, and numerous talk shows. When she attended the prestigious alternative media festival South by Southwest in 2013, six hundred fans waited in line for hours to take a selfie with her.

This social media star had a merchandise line that included nine hundred items such as T-shirts, mugs, stuffed toys, a video game, and an annual calendar that featured photos of her. Her internet celebrity helped push her 2016 book to number three on the *New York Times* Best Sellers list. After racking up billions of hits and attracting millions of fans, she became the official representative for Friskies. This was a perfect brand for her to endorse—the internet celebrity was Grumpy Cat, a brown and white cat with a permanently frowny face caused by feline dwarfism.

By the time Grumpy Cat died in 2019, she had achieved a level of social media stardom that millions of humans can only dream of. By some estimates,

Grumpy Cat's owner, Tabatha Bundesen, earned over $100 million from her famous feline. Like other internet stars and influencers, Grumpy Cat used social media to bring in money from a number of sources. Bundesen's early revenue came from sponsored ads on Grumpy Cat YouTube videos. Advertisers paid to display pre-roll ads that play before a video starts and also sponsored banner and sidebar ads that are visible at all times. Google, which owns YouTube, paid Bundesen through its AdSense program, which tallies every click on each video. While figures vary, AdSense generally pays an average of 18 cents per video view, or $18 per thousand. Google keeps 45 percent, so a YouTuber earns a little less than $10 for every thousand views. Grumpy Cat's original YouTube video from 2013 received over 22 million

Grumpy Cat was an internet celebrity with millions of fans. By some estimates, Grumpy Cat earned over $100 million for her owner.

views, which means Bundesen earned over $220,000 from that one video alone. And several dozen videos of the cat were uploaded later, many of which have more than 1 million views.

Social Media Influencers

There are more famous humans than famous cats on social media, but the revenue stream for people and pets is the same. And those looking at their Instagram feed for more than ten seconds will see some major celebrity, microcelebrity, or vlogger promoting a product. Promoters might be fashion bloggers, gym instructors, musicians, chefs, or even woodworkers, but they all have something in common: they are social media influencers. They are paid by advertising agencies to hype products on social media sites.

The reason influencers are inescapable on social media is because they are convincing spokespersons. According to the influencer marketing website Mediakix, 60 percent of YouTube viewers have made a purchase based on an influencer's advice. This fact has propelled 72 percent of major brands, including Nissan, Uber, Revlon, and Old Navy, to significantly increase their influencer marketing budgets since 2018. These major corporations work with influencer marketing directors at advertising agencies to hire Instagram stars, bloggers, YouTubers, and TikTokers who can create social media buzz around their client's products.

Marketers are most interested in social media influencers who have already built their own brand online and have a large audience that follows their videos, photos, blogs, and other posts. However, an influencer does not need to be as famous as Grumpy Cat to attract attention from advertisers. Influencer marketing director Joe Gagliese explains how social media personalities appeal to select markets and often have a powerful influence even if that market is relatively small. "A middle-aged audience is . . . a valuable demographic," Gagliese states. "We work with this one influencer, Gerry Brooks, for example, who is a school principal and a Facebook personality with almost 1 million likes; 90 percent of his followers are women who work as teachers, and are 35 and up." Brooks makes videos and does public speaking tours that are aimed at inspiring teachers and educational administrators. "That is a unique, and lucrative, audience,"[4] Gagliese says.

Gagliese is the cofounder of Viral Nation, a marketing agency that represents over ten thousand influencers—including PewDiePie, one of the most-followed people on YouTube, with 120 million subscribers. PewDiePie was born in Sweden in 1989, and his real name is Felix Kjellberg. He began posting videos to YouTube in 2010 before the concept of social media influencer existed. PewDiePie initially worked at a hot dog stand and spent his free time posting YouTube videos with color commentary on video games. When PewDiePie made a play-by-play video of the popular *Minecraft* game, his antics and comments racked up 12 million views. The following year when his YouTube channel reached sixty thousand subscribers, PewDiePie quit selling hot dogs.

Four years into his career, PewDiePie earned an estimated $7.4 million, more than double his income from the previous year. PewDiePie ended his video posts with a pumping, clenched-fist

Going Live for Tips

The concept of patrons providing monetary tips to social media stars began with the fund-raising service Patreon, which remains popular on YouTube. Those who seek donations on TikTok for their lip-synching, dancing, singing, comedy, and acrobatics have their own system for collecting tips. Anyone with at least one thousand followers can use TikTok's Go Live feature to livestream. TikTok users can buy virtual currency in the form of digital coins. Prices vary depending on the number purchased: 100 coins were 99 cents in 2020. Users store their virtual coins in an online wallet and can give them to TikTokers during livestream performances. (TikTok keeps around 20 percent.) TikTokers see Go Live as a great way to stay connected with followers and reap rewards from fans. Performers can redeem their tips at any time, up to $1,000 a day.

Felix Kjellberg (on left), known as PewDiePie, has 120 million followers on YouTube.

gesture he called a Brofist. In 2015 he turned this into a lucra-tive video game, *PewDiePie: Legend of the Brofist*. The five-dollar mobile app was a hit among his fans, whom he called his Bro Army. A second successful video game, *PewDiePie's Tuber Sim-ulator*, was released in 2016.

PewDiePie possessed a near-mythical formula that helped him grow from a minor YouTube publisher to a social media celebrity. Like most social media celebrities and influencers,

PewDiePie is entertaining and informative. He is charismatic, attractive, and photogenic. PewDiePie's camera presence gives fans the feeling that he is their best friend. The Bro Army thinks he is funny and engaging. His videos are high quality, on topic, and not rambling or boring; he often drops in clever pop culture references and humorous comments. As fan Vicenzo Tsai writes, PewDiePie comes across as authentic and relatable: "He is very dedicated to his fans as he constantly provided his fans an opportunity to express themselves through his various media channels. He produced videos almost weekly just for his many fans which increased his popularity as most of his fans were youth which have great accessibility to social technology."[6]

"[PewDiePie] produced videos almost weekly just for his many fans which increased his popularity as most of his fans . . . have great accessibility to social technology."[5]

—Vicenzo Tsai, PewDiePie fan

One of the revenue streams social media stars like PewDiePie can tap into is the online fund-raising service Patreon. Followers, called patrons, give their favorite social media star donations on a regular basis to support current or future projects. In exchange, patrons often receive behind the scenes material, exclusive content, and access to early releases. YouTubers might also personally interact with patrons via text or email. YouTuber Evan Edinger explains how patronage works. "Think of it as an online tip jar," he says. "If you really like [the videos] and want to support them then you can pay something like a dollar per video, or a dollar per month. . . . I've had a patreon [account] for about a year now and those viewers get to watch my videos a bit early and sometimes they ask questions."[6]

While the Bro Army might love PewDiePie, he has generated his fair share of controversy for using racial slurs, making crude anti-Semitic jokes, and publishing expletive-laden rants. But the controversies did not drive

"Think of [Patreon] as an online tip jar. . . . If you really like [the videos] and want to support them then you can pay something like a dollar per video, or a dollar per month."[6]

—Evan Edinger, YouTuber

The Hype House

When social media stars and influencers live together and collaborate to create content, their residence is called a collab house. One of the earliest collab houses, the O2L House, was set up in 2014 by a YouTube channel called Our Second Life. By 2020 the collab house trend was adopted by a new generation—TikTok influencers who set up content shops in some of Los Angeles's toniest neighborhoods, including Bel Air, Beverly Hills, Studio City, and Hollywood.

The Hype House is a collab house founded by TikTok stars Thomas Petrou and Lilhuddy (Chase Hudson). It is home to four live-in residents and nineteen collaborators who often stay there on weekends. The first Hype House photoshoot in December 2019 began trending almost immediately. Within a month, videos bearing the #hypehouse hashtag accumulated nearly 100 million views on TikTok.

Hype House is located in a Spanish-style mansion with many features that make it perfect for TikTok video shoots. It has good natural light, features a lot of open space, and is in a gated community, which prevents fans from swarming the place. There are plenty of giant mirrors, a sweeping staircase, huge marble bathrooms, lush green lawns, and a large pool to provide backdrops for TikTok videos. While collaborators can entertain guests, Hype House is not a party house. People are expected to create loads of content every day. As Petrou says, "It's 24/7 here. Last night we posted at 2 a.m. There's probably 100 TikToks made here per day. At minimum."

Quoted in Taylor Lorenz, "Hype House and the Los Angeles TikTok Mansion Gold Rush," *New York Times*, January 3, 2020. www.nytimes.com.

---

away fans. In 2019 PewDiePie became the first individual YouTuber to hit the 100 million subscriber mark. As the tenth anniversary of his YouTube career neared in January 2020, PewDiePie had earned an estimated $40 million endorsing products, appearing in films, releasing video games, and even producing a few top ten records. Whether by accident or chance, PewDiePie has become a pioneering social media star.

TikTokers Take Over

PewDiePie's success as a YouTuber and a businessperson spawned millions of imitators who tried to follow the same path to success. But social media is in constant flux. By the time PewDiePie decided to take a break in 2019, YouTubers were being eclipsed by TikTokers, a new generation fluent in creating videos for TikTok. This game-changing app is used to share fifteen- to sixty-second videos that feature lip-synching, dancing, comedy, and various challenges. While TikTok is not as well established as YouTube, by 2020 it was a viral sensation.

TikTok is an international phenomenon; the app was designed in Beijing, China, by a tech company called ByteDance. The TikTok app was launched internationally in 2017, and by 2020 it had been downloaded 1.5 billion times. According to the mobile intelligence firm Sensor Tower, TikTok was available in 154 countries in 2020 and had about 800 million monthly users, compared to 2 billion on YouTube. Around 466 million TikTok users live in India, 173 million are in China, and 60 million reside in the United States.

TikTok uses sophisticated artificial intelligence algorithms to suggest new videos based on past behavior. This key feature is known as the For You Page, or #fyp in TikTok lingo. Users are presented with videos that might interest them based on their viewing history. Anyone's random video on TikTok can pop up on screens all over the world. If the video is clever and engaging, the creator might become an instant viral sensation, at least for a day or two. The For You Page gives average users a chance for stardom and makes the app irresistible. Journalist Georgia Bynum attests, "Tik Tok is its own little world, and let me tell you, it is FAR too easy to get sucked in."[7]

Bynum's observation is backed up by facts. The average TikTok user spends about an hour on the app each day. While parents might object, this type of obsession is a marketer's dream. Sixty percent of TikTokers are from Generation Z, a cohort of 74 million young people that advertisers view as trendsetters. Around 40 percent of TikTokers are male, while females make up 60 percent of users. It is little wonder that TikTok was paying popular influencers $500 each in 2020 just to sign up and create new content for the app. This incentive was fueling TikTok's growth, attracting billions of dollars from marketers, and pulling influencers away from YouTube.

Top TikTokers

Most popular TikTok stars have not matched the popularity of PewDiePie. But some TikTokers have attracted millions of followers with their talent, good looks, and authenticity. And some who began their careers as TikTokers have gone on to find success in other entertainment fields. Loren Gray exemplifies this trend. In 2020 the seventeen-year-old singer was the most-followed person on TikTok, with 39 million followers. Gray began her rise to the top of social media stardom in 2015 as a Muser, someone who posted content to the short-video platform Musical.ly. (All videos from this site were moved to TikTok in 2018 after Musical.ly was purchased by ByteDance.) Gray's model-like good looks, perky dance moves, and energetic lip-synching also attracted 18 million followers on Instagram and 3.5 million on YouTube. Gray is more than a lip-synch star, however. She also sings and writes songs. She was able to use her social media popularity to land a record deal with Virgin Records in 2018. Gray released five singles with accompanying videos; her third video, *Queen*, was viewed more than 12 million times on YouTube, while her 2019 song "Anti-Everything" was nominated for the Social Star Award at the 2019 iHeartRadio Music Awards.

Social media personality and actress Baby Ariel was the second-most popular TikToker in 2020, with 29 million followers. Baby Ariel was fifteen in 2015 when she began posting lip-synch videos to Musical.ly. She gained national media attention for launching the high-profile campaign against online bullying called #ArielMovement. The campaign, which earned the Innovator Honor from the *Wall Street Journal*, proved to Baby Ariel's followers that she was a sincere, honest person who deserved their attention. By the time she was seventeen, Baby Ariel had assembled an audience of 30 million followers and was featured in televised segments on CNN and *60 Minutes*. This led to a contract with the prestigious talent agency Creative Artists Agency and the release of several songs, including "Aww" (2017) and "Say It" (2019). Baby Ariel's success led journalist Ken Scrudato to call her "the paradigm modern media star."[8] By 2020 her short videos had earned a total of 1.7 billion hearts—the TikTok equivalent of likes.

Brand Partnerships and Sponsored Posts

In addition to promoting themselves and their talents, social media stars earn big money from brand partnerships. Producers of consumer goods, or brands, partner with the stars to promote lipstick, candy bars, clothing, electronics, and other products in their videos. Once again Loren Gray provides a good example of how this works. In addition to producing music and dance videos, Gray partners with hair and makeup companies to make tutorials for YouTube. She earns up to $175,000 for each video, where she can be seen using one of her partners' brands.

Social media stars also create what are called sponsored posts, which might be considered short commercials produced by influencers rather than by professional ad production companies. Product manufacturers are especially eager to back TikTokers because some of their sponsored posts can go viral. This is what happened in 2019 with Mucinex, a brand of cold and flu medicine. Mucinex paid the brother-sister duo OurFire (with 5.6 million followers) to create a video that showed them lying in bed, both suffering from a cold. The camera makes a quick cut to the Mucinex bottle and features shots of OurFire getting dressed up and looking great on their way to a nightclub. The influencer video delivered a message that touched off a viral ad campaign, racking up nearly 1 million hearts by 2020.

OurFire earned an estimated $75,000 for the sponsored post. While that might sound like a lot of money for the influencers, it is a bargain for large corporations. Producing a professional ad for network television can cost hundreds of thousands of dollars. In 2020 the cost to run a single thirty-second spot on a popular show like *This Is Us* or *The Masked Singer* was $200,000.

Social media stars can earn big money promoting consumer goods such as cosmetics, clothing, candy bars, and electronics.

Little wonder that McDonald's, Target, Coca-Cola, and dozens of other major brands are altering their marketing strategies to favor TikTokers. As TikTok comedy creator Drea Knows Best explains, "All the creators on the app have very loyal fans. If they say, 'Hey, guys, I'm partnering with Burger King, everyone go to Burger King and buy a burger,' they will go to Burger King and buy a burger because they trust the influencers on TikTok and they're loyal to them. It's just phenomenal."[9] The statistics back Drea's assertion. According to the marketing firm CivicScience, 15 percent of Americans purchased a product or service in 2019 because an influencer used it or promoted it on social media.

Collaborations at Collab Houses

Tal Fishman views the marketing power of TikTok from the perspective of a successful YouTube comedy creator. Fishman launched his Reaction Time channel in 2015 and amassed over 14 million subscribers while earning millions of dollars from advertisers. In 2020, at age twenty-three, Fishman did not wish to compete with teenagers on TikTok. This led him to cofound TalentX Entertainment, a TikTok talent management agency that would serve as a launchpad for brand partnerships, merchandising, live events, and even television and film development.

TalentX is run out of a Hollywood mansion known as the Sway House. Six of the agency's top influencer clients live in the house and collaborate on videos. They pay no rent but must meet content quotas, producing a fixed number of videos each week. TalentX cofounder Jason Wilhelm explains, "You wake up and they're just filming. You walk in the house and they're filming. It's pretty remarkable."[10]

Sway House is part of the collab house (collaboration house) trend that YouTubers started in 2014. In collab houses content creators are in constant contact, day and night. They bounce ideas off one another and pool their talents and resources to produce

"Power players on these platforms . . . lift each other up. . . . 'Elevate others to elevate yourself' is a saying, and it really rings true with this new generation of TikTokers."[11]

—Sam Sheffer, YouTuber

videos that are presumably better than those that they would make alone. Collaborators cross-promote one another on their personal accounts and on the collab account. They also hone their teamwork skills and provide mutual emotional support to one another. YouTuber Sam Sheffer says, "It's a brilliant move for power players on these platforms to lift each other up. . . . 'Elevate others to elevate yourself' is a saying, and it really rings true with this new generation of TikTokers."[11]

Beyond lifting one another up, the Sway collaborators have access to Hollywood talent agents and casting directors. Television networks and film producers have come to understand that TikTok is producing the next generation of actors, singers, and cultural influencers. And Sway House is only one of several collab houses located in Los Angeles. Hype House, in a huge Spanish-style mansion, is home to four influencers and open to nineteen others who come to produce content every day—including some who are still in high school and live with their parents.

Everyone Wants to Be an Influencer

It is not hard to understand the appeal of TikTok. The app was designed to allow almost anyone to go viral. Dancer Charli D'Amelio, who started using TikTok in 2019, exemplifies this concept. She quickly amassed nearly 24 million followers and appeared in a Super Bowl ad less than a year later. And as Bynum writes, this type of instant fame has a special appeal to Gen Zers. "We are a generation that has been demanded to perform. We have to stand out, be unique, be funny, be pretty, be something. And Tik Tok is a place where anyone can be anything. Social media has

"We have to stand out, be unique, be funny, be pretty, be something. And Tik Tok is a place where anyone can be anything."[12]

—Georgia Bynum, journalist

taken over our lives in a way that is so scary but makes so much sense. We crave attention and validation. We are putting on a show."[12]

While YouTubers and Musers led the way, TikTok provides the promise of the greatest rewards for the least amount of effort. TikTok lets users shine a spotlight on themselves and attract attention for their individual talents. As youth marketing director Madison Bregman explains, "Every single kid wants to be an entrepreneur or an influencer."[13] While not everyone can be the next Loren Gray—or the owner of a money-making grumpy cat—the world is waiting for the next big star to take on the TikTok crowd and create a fifteen-second show that will light up #fyp and rack up the hearts.

Chapter Two

Mainstream Social Media Superstars

YouTubers, TikTokers, and the Instafamous might register millions of subscribers and rack up billions of views, but the large majority of people do not follow gamers, fashion vloggers, amateur comedians, and other social media stars. People like PewDiePie and Loren Gray do not have the kind of widespread name recognition afforded to popular musicians and actors. Mainstream recording artists like country singer Kane Brown and rapper Cardi B began their careers as social media stars on Instagram, SoundCloud, Facebook, and other sites. Before they were signed to major record labels, they posted content that grabbed viewers' attention, generated likes and shares, and attracted notice from well-connected promoters and record producers.

Even after attaining mainstream success, those who launched their careers on social media continue to build their following by connecting with followers on a regular basis. They use social media to post picture-perfect portraits, clips of backstage antics, and concert videos. They also act as brand influencers for themselves, informing fans about their upcoming concert tours, record releases, and television appearances.

From Facebook to Number One

Kane Brown has set sales records on the *Billboard* country charts and has taken home numerous awards for his music. He launched a successful mainstream career as a country artist through the skillful use of Facebook. Brown was twenty when he began his career in 2014 as one of millions of amateur musicians who posted informal videos of themselves on Facebook. Brown first used his iPhone to record himself strumming the guitar and singing songs by popular country artists. The sound quality was poor, but Brown's honeyed baritone voice and smooth country delivery shone through. His first Facebook videos went viral, and he quickly racked up over 7 million views. Brown used his social media success to launch a crowdfunding campaign on Kickstarter, raising enough money to finance production of a six-song extended play (EP) called *Closer*. When the EP was completed, Brown generated interest by posting short song clips with iTunes links, which influenced fans to purchase the record.

Brown is multiracial. His mother is white, and his father is half black and half Cherokee Indian. The songs on *Closer* revealed Brown's personal struggles with racism growing up. While the singer was nervous about revealing intimate details of his life, many of his followers identified with his lyrics. The sharing culture on social media helped *Closer* debut at number twenty-two on the Top Country Album Chart. The EP quickly jumped to number forty on the *Billboard* 200.

In 2015 Brown posted a video to YouTube of him singing a new song, "Used to Love You Sober," in a North Carolina bar. The video received 11 million views in two weeks, which helped push the song to the top of the sales charts. Brown's social media popularity attracted interest from a number of record companies, and in 2016 he was signed by Sony Music Nashville. By that time Brown had amassed more than 3 million followers on Facebook, while his performance videos and previews generated more than 100 million views and shares. Brown credited his strong social media following for his success:

My fans have always been supportive, and have always been there for me. They are always there, and sharing everything that I put up. When I release something, they will be the first to go get it. They'll tag me or share me, and really try to get out there and spread the word and let people know about my songs and my albums. Without them, I wouldn't have had half the success that we have had, and I have to give props to them, and let them know I love them.[14]

Mainstream recording artists such as Kane Brown (pictured) began their careers as social media stars on Instagram, SoundCloud, Facebook, and other sites.

Cardi B's Influence

The raunchy rap music created by Cardi B would never be mistaken for Kane Brown's smooth country stylings. But Brown and Cardi B can both credit their rise from poverty and obscurity to their influence on social media. Cardi B began her career as a stripper in 2011 before most people had ever heard of social media influencers. At the time, there were few online personalities who promoted themselves and their brands while racking up clicks and likes on Instagram, Twitter, and Facebook. But Cardi B's popularity as a dancer helped her develop a list of admirers such as local bartenders, bouncers, and club regulars. By 2013 she had thousands of followers on Instagram and Tumblr who loved her attention-grabbing memes, selfies, and videos. Like many social media stars, Cardi B was a natural on camera. She spoke directly into her phone and showed off her vibrant personality and augmented curves while reeling off hilarious, obscenity-laden observations at a hundred miles an hour.

> "[My fans will] tag me or share me, and really try to get out there and spread the word and let people know about my songs and my albums."[14]
>
> —Kane Brown, singer

At the time, most social media influencers were somewhat careful about what they said. But Cardi B had no filter. She gossiped about her childhood poverty, her sex life, and the lowlife customers she met working in a strip bar. And Cardi B was not one of those Instafamous celebrities who spent hours before the mirror applying makeup and ensuring every hair was in place. Oftentimes she looked like she just rolled out of bed, without makeup and sometimes without much clothing.

By 2014 Cardi B's account grew to 1 million as she attracted throngs of young women who were eager to hear her trash-talking dating advice. Taking on the role of a New York City social media celebrity, Cardi B began hosting club gatherings in which patrons paid admission to hang out with her in a nightclub. This attracted the attention of promoters and advertisers, who paid Cardi B to promote their brand, wear their fashions, and mention their products in her posts.

Cardi B was a microcelebrity in 2015, but she became a macrocelebrity after she was cast on season six of the long-running VH1 reality TV show *Love & Hip-Hop: New York*. Cardi B was originally set to play a minor role as a struggling stripper. But her years of practice making viral videos full of spontaneous outbursts, whip-smart wit, and revealing outfits made her the breakout cast member of *Love & Hip-Hop: New York*. Cardi B was breaking the internet with every new episode of *Love & Hip-Hop*. Her memorable scenes and laugh-out-loud put-downs were turned into memes and gifs by fans.

In 2016 Cardi B leveraged her social media stardom into a successful mainstream rap career. When she released her first mixtape, *Gangsta Bitch Music, Vol. 1*, it reached number twenty on the *Billboard* Top Rap Albums Chart. In 2017, after releasing her second mixtape, *Gangsta Bitch Music, Vol. 2*, Cardi B landed a multimillion-dollar record contract with Atlantic Records.

While few strippers become top-trending Instagram influencers—and fewer still become television stars—Cardi B was one of the first to prove that nontraditional celebrities can be highly influential. Cardi B's brand partnership with the clothing line Fashion Nova proves this point. Fashion Nova's popularity skyrocketed after it hired Cardi B to promote its clothing line in her Instagram videos. Likewise, Cardi B's career received a boost from Fashion Nova. Users of the clothing line's website could click through to Cardi B's Instagram, which helped increase the number of followers on her account. In 2018, after achieving mainstream superstar status, she launched her own brand, the Fashion Nova x Cardi B clothing line.

Cashing In with Cupcakes and Cashmere

Most social media celebrities will never become as popular as Cardi B. But there are others who have used their influence as Cardi B has to create their own successful product lines. Fash-

Jessica Alba: Telling Personalized Stories

Actor Jessica Alba has been called a hybrid of an A-list celebrity and mega influencer. Alba's appearance in the 2005 superhero movie *Fantastic Four* helped make her an international movie star. Between appearing in hit TV shows, action movies, rom-coms, and thrillers, Alba launched the Honest Company in 2011. The company sells eco-friendly baby, self-care, home, health, and beauty products.

Alba says the mission of the Honest Company is to empower families to lead happy, healthy lives, and she wants to offer millennial moms trusted, natural products. To ensure the success of the company, Alba acted as a brand ambassador for her new company, promoting it to her millions of followers on Instagram, Twitter, and other social media platforms. Alba's influence brought attention—and customers—to the Honest Company. The brand continued to grow by generating real connections to its customers through influencer marketing. While Alba remained the face of the Honest Company, real mothers, who might be called microcelebrities, were enlisted to tell their compelling, personalized stories on social media. Moms who had ten thousand to fifty thousand Instagram followers were enlisted to post baby photos and comments about Honest Company products. This helped the company attract more than 2 million followers on Facebook, 1 million on Instagram, and 100,000 on Twitter. The personalized marketing also helped make Alba one of the richest women in the world. In 2017 the Honest Company had a value of $1 billion.

ion and lifestyle blogger Emily Schuman accomplished this with her *Cupcakes and Cashmere* blog. Schuman was no stranger to fashion and celebrity influence. She began her career as a media professional working for *Teen Vogue*. Like Cardi B, Schuman understood the power of social media to promote brands long before it was trendy.

Schuman was twenty-five when she launched *Cupcakes and Cashmere* in 2008. She had been posting anonymous restaurant reviews to Yelp, which inspired her to start a blog so she could write about her two favorite topics, food and fashion. "I missed that feeling of doing something creative, and that's how I began," she says. "I didn't want to turn it into a business, but I wanted to create something I was proud of."[15]

Schuman promoted herself as the millennials' answer to lifestyle and decorating icon Martha Stewart. *Cupcakes and Cashmere* was professionally designed to resemble the glossy lifestyle magazine *Martha Stewart Living*. The blog features stylish fashions, recipes, decorating tips, and do-it-yourself projects. By 2013 *Cupcakes and Cashmere* was attracting more than 120,000 daily visitors. This led the Los Angeles–based blogger to publish *Cup-*

The glossy lifestyle magazine Martha Stewart Living *became the model for Emily Schuman's lifestyle blog,* Cupcakes and Cashmere.

cakes and Cashmere: A Guide for Defining Your Style, Reinventing Your Space, and Entertaining with Ease, a best seller in 2013.

While there are thousands of lifestyle blogs on the internet, Schuman had a personal touch, speaking to readers as a friend. She promoted the site every day by posting lavish photos of food and fashion on Twitter and Instagram. Her efforts attracted major fashion brands that were excited to reach her thousands of loyal readers. Schuman promotes products for Coach, Forever 21, Juicy Couture, and Estee Lauder with photos, videos, product reviews, and interactive ads on her website. The clicks, likes, and shares on *Cashmere and Cupcakes* translated into hundreds of thousands of dollars in income for Schuman.

In 2015 Schuman published her second book, *Cupcakes and Cashmere at Home*. She also produced her own clothing line in collaboration with the fashion brand BB Dakota. By 2017 *Cupcakes and Cashmere* had over 1 million monthly visitors, and Schuman's blog had grown into what journalist Vivienne Decker calls "an aspirational, girl-next-door lifestyle brand."[16] To further promote her brand, Schuman launched an e-commerce platform, where fans could shop for her designer brands as well as two hundred of her favorite home, fashion, and gift products.

Schuman's expertise in social media transformed her from an unnamed food reviewer into a mainstream fashion influencer. She offers this advice to those looking to follow in her footsteps:

> "Start for the right reasons. . . . I simply shared things I was passionate about and other people took notice."[17]
>
> —Emily Schuman, founder of *Cupcakes and Cashmere*

Start for the right reasons. Back when I first began *Cupcakes and Cashmere*, a career in blogging wasn't really a thing, I simply shared things I was passionate about and other people took notice. I think that level of authenticity is the cornerstone for whatever you create. Beyond that, develop a unique voice, take high-quality photographs, have a clean site layout, post often, and interact with your readers.[17]

The Goop Effect

While some social media stars like Schuman have become widely known celebrities, some film and television celebrities have used these platforms to increase their influencer status and make big money. Gwyneth Paltrow was one of the first award-winning actors to use their social media star power to launch a successful online company. In 2008 Paltrow's career was on an upswing after she starred in the blockbuster super-hero movie *Iron Man*. However, at the time, Paltrow was generating as much media coverage for her lifestyle website, Goop. Paltrow says she fashioned the name around her initials and the fact that many successful internet companies have double Os in their name.

Goop began as a weekly email newsletter with a new age slogan, "Nourish the Inner Aspect."[18] Paltrow filled her newsletters with what she called her collection of experiences that included recipes, health and fashion advice, motherhood tips, and recommendations for extremely expensive clothing, including $935 pants from Rag & Bone. Critics mercilessly ridiculed Paltrow for curating products and experiences that could only be enjoyed by the ultrarich and privileged. But Paltrow said the negative publicity helped her newsletter. She quickly attracted an audience of young women who were interested in her aspirational lifestyle brand.

Paltrow launched the Goop website in coordination with an email blast that explained, "Whether you want a good place to eat in London, some advice on where to stay in Austin, the recipe I made up this week, or some thoughts from one of my sages, Goop is a little bit of everything that makes up my life."[19] By 2012 the Goop newsletter had seven hundred thousand subscribers, leading Paltrow to open an online shop selling makeup, skin care products, fashions, fragrances, and other goods.

Goop grew into a multimillion-dollar enterprise selling bizarre and absurdly overpriced objects, such as $27 bottles of Psychic Vampire Repellent and $244 toothpaste tube squeezers. These products, along with Paltrow's sketchy new-age health advice, generated scorn in the media. But Paltrow called the internet vitriol "cultural firestorms" while claiming "I can monetize those eyeballs."[20]

Paltrow certainly did monetize the controversies surrounding Goop. By 2018 Goop was worth more than $250 million. The company had eight hundred thousand followers on Instagram, five hundred thousand on Facebook, and a strong social media presence on Twitter, YouTube, and Pinterest. Marketing expert Liz Alton explains why Goop became successful:

> **"I can monetize those eyeballs."[20]**
>
> —Gwyneth Paltrow, actor and Goop entrepreneur

> Its social [media] channels show minimal selling. Instead, it publishes a number of lifestyle pieces. It's got recipe videos, blogs, wellness tips, travel guides, and more. Product mentions are done tastefully, using posts that still have the lifestyle vibe, with a simple "products mentioned" section below. [And it] seems as though each channel is uniquely curated. You aren't going to check out its Facebook page and see the exact same images as what's on its Instagram page. It also isn't overdoing the hashtags on Instagram.[21]

Paltrow expanded her company's reach by launching *The goop Podcast* in 2018. With a weekly audience averaging around 350,000 listeners, the show consistently ranks at the top of the Apple Podcast charts. Snippets of the podcast are shared on Instagram. Goop also has a Spotify channel that shares jams and playlists users might be interested in.

Paltrow's success is credited with inspiring other celebrities to launch lifestyle companies online. Hilary Duff, Selma Blair, Kate Hudson, and Jessica Alba regularly post sponsored content on their social media accounts and have set up online shops to sell products to fans.

The Gen Z Billionaire Influencer

Goop helped make Paltrow one of the wealthiest women in the world, but her influence has been eclipsed by a reality television star. In 2020 Kylie Jenner was considered one of the most influential people on social media. She was only nine years old when she made her television debut as the youngest sister on the TV show *Keeping Up with the Kardashians*. The show, which premiered in 2007, follows the lives of sisters Kourtney, Kim, and Khloé Kardashian and their half sisters, Kylie and Kendall Jenner. *Keeping Up with the Kardashians* has been consistently panned by television reviewers as a show about sisters with no apparent talents who are famous for being famous. But the program was an instant hit, making household names out of Kylie Jenner and the rest of her family. *Keeping Up with the Kardashians* began a new season in 2020.

Over the years Jenner grew from a shy kid into an attractive young woman with a great fashion sense. By the time she was fifteen, Jenner had signed promotional deals with clothing companies PacSun, Steve Madden, and Topshop and with the candymaker Sugar Factory. And while everyone in the entire Kardashian-Jenner family had millions of followers on social media, Kylie stood out from the rest, with 60 million followers on Facebook, Twitter, Instagram, and Snapchat. Jenner also released a $2.99-a-month app that generated 1.75 million downloads the first week.

"Everything I do, I always start these huge trends."[22]

—Kylie Jenner, reality TV star

Jenner attracted widespread attention in 2015 for her lip augmentation, a surgical procedure in which fat is injected into the lips to enlarge them. Jenner took advantage of the publicity by launching a lipstick line on Instagram called the Kylie Lip Kit. The twenty-nine-dollar kits, which consist of lip liner and liquid lipstick, sold out online in less than one minute. When Jenner made *Time* magazine's 30 Most Influential Teens of 2015 list, she said, "Everything I do, I always start these huge trends."[22] In 2016 the direct-to-consumer Kylie

How Kylie Jenner Captured Social Media

Kylie Jenner was born into wealth and grew up in public on the trendy TV reality show *Keeping Up with the Kardashians*. But there was no guarantee that Jenner's company, Kylie Cosmetics, would make her a billionaire at age twenty-one. Those who have observed Jenner's success say that her skillful use of social media helped her build a cosmetics empire in an incredibly short period of time.

Jenner achieved instant recognition because she stood out from the crowd. Although she was the youngest member in a family of glamorous women, Jenner found a niche that distinguished her from the others by focusing on her passion. She was obsessed with applying lipstick in a way that would give her lips a fuller, pouty look. Jenner's fascination with the perfect lip look was obvious in her social media posts. The excitement translated to followers who eagerly purchase her lip kits.

Jenner understands that she needs to keep her audience captivated when making social media posts. While she posts professional beauty shots to sell Kylie Cosmetics, she also posts no-makeup selfies and risqué outtakes from photo shoots. This helps provide Jenner a feel of authenticity. Her postings about her everyday life, including photos of her baby, offer fans a peek behind the curtain. Jenner's followers feel a close connection that they might not have otherwise. By finding a niche, focusing on her obses sion, and projecting an authentic image, Jenner has become one of the most influential celebrities of her generation.

Cosmetics makeup line grew to include eyeshadows, blushes, makeup brushes, and highlighters, or kylighters, as Jenner called them. This business expansion generated $420 million for Jenner before her cosmetics venture was even two years old.

In 2018 Jenner appeared on the cover of *Forbes* magazine for its "America's Women Billionaires" issue. The magazine said the rapid growth of Kylie Cosmetics made Jenner the twenty-seventh-richest self-made woman in the United States. With a net worth of more than $900 million, Jenner was not yet a billionaire. But the following year Jenner's wealth had increased to the point that *Forbes* named her the world's youngest billionaire ever. At age twenty-one Jenner was also the first self-made Gen Z billionaire.

Some complained that Jenner could hardly be called "self-made" since she was born into a wealthy, famous family. Whatever the case, none could deny that Jenner's expert use of Instagram, Facebook, and other platforms had made her incredibly rich. In 2020 Jenner had a total of 175 million followers on all her social media platforms and was one of the top ten most-followed people on Instagram. This allowed her to charge $1 million for a single post promoting a product. As Jenner explains, "It's the power of social media. I had such a strong reach before I was able to start anything."[23]

Jenner's power was on display in 2018 after Snapchat redesigned its app. She thought the new layout was too confusing to navigate. Jenner tweeted her displeasure to her 24 million Twitter followers: "Sooo does anyone else not open Snapchat anymore?

Kylie Jenner (second from left) joined other members of Keeping Up with the Kardashians for a 2008 photo. She was just a kid and relatively unknown when the show began in 2007 but now she has 175 million followers on social media.

Or is it just me . . . ugh this is so sad."[24] Soon after Jenner's tweet the stock price of Snapchat plunged, wiping out $850 million of the company's market value.

Racking Up Followers

Jenner found a way to profit from Snapchat's pain. Within twenty-four hours of making headlines for crashing the company's stock, Jenner provided her followers with a peek at three new shades of her sold-out Lip Kits that would soon be available once again to the public. But because of her attitude about Snapchat, she made the announcement on Instagram.

As Jenner and countless others have shown, it is easy for the already famous to rack up millions of followers. And microcelebrities can achieve macrocelebrity status, as Cardi B did, by using social media to heighten their influence, gain mainstream fame, and generate vast sums of money. When everyone, everywhere, is connected to everyone else on social media, the biggest market place on earth is only a few clicks away. And as Paltrow proved, there are billions of eyeballs waiting to be monetized.

Chapter Three

Reality Check

Conduct an internet search with the words "every kid wants to be a YouTuber" and hundreds of articles pop up quoting polls, surveys, and various experts. Each article points out that millions of kids would love to earn millions of dollars as YouTubers. And there is little doubt that life as a highly paid social media star seems like a lot of fun. Eight-year-old Ryan Kaji was the top YouTube earner in 2019. His toy-review channel Ryan's World, with nearly 24 million subscribers, brought in over $26 million. Other top earners, such as Evan Fong, DanTDM, and Markiplier, earned over $11 million each playing video games.

Getting paid millions to post YouTube videos sounds like an amazing job. But anyone planning a career as a YouTuber, TikToker, or other social media influencer needs to conduct a reality check. The odds of becoming the next Ryan Kaji or DanTDM are about the same as becoming the next Beyoncé or Billie Eilish. While millions start with big dreams and work to achieve fame as social media influencers, they find it is difficult to attract viewers.

Against the Odds

YouTube figures show that it takes an average of six months to gain one hundred subscribers on a YouTube channel. Nine out of ten channels never manage to attract five thousand subscribers. This means wannabe influencers cannot participate in YouTube's AdSense program; a channel must have at least one thousand subscribers and accrue four thousand hours of watch time over the course of twelve months to earn money. Since it takes an average of one hundred thousand views to attract one thousand subscribers, channels with low numbers never earn a profit. As a result, one in every four channels is abandoned within three months.

The competition to attract views and subscribers is fierce. Five hundred hours of video footage are uploaded to the platform every minute of every day. Five hundred hours equals twenty-one days; even with 2 billion people logging in to YouTube every month, most of that footage will never be seen by more than a few people.

Even though 2 billion viewers log in every month, most YouTube videos will never be seen by more than a few people.

"You can have half a million followers on YouTube and still be working at Starbucks."[25]

—Alice Marwick, communications professor

In 2018 German science professor Mathias Bärtl analyzed YouTube statistics and discovered that 85 percent of viewer traffic went to just 3 percent of the channels. The top 3 percent of creators earned the bulk of YouTube's advertising payouts. According to Bärtl, the other 97 percent of wannabe YouTubers who participated in AdSense earned less than $12,140 annually. This is considered a poverty wage for a single person in the United States. Even those with 1.4 million monthly viewers only earned about $16,800 annually. Communications professor Alice Marwick notes, "You can have half a million followers on YouTube and still be working at Starbucks."[25]

Giving Up a Job—and Privacy

Whatever their earnings, hopeful social media stars must invest time and money. Cheap-looking, shaky videos do not attract subscribers. Equipment like a good video camera, a tripod to hold it, a good microphone, and lights and light stands can cost anywhere from $500 to $5,000. Content producers also need an up-to-date computer that can run that latest video editing software.

The demands associated with being a part-time YouTuber or TikToker can affect individuals' careers, whether they work at a coffee shop or anywhere else. Filming, uploading, monetizing, and marketing every video requires a time commitment. Some quit their jobs or give up on school to pursue their social media dreams. But there is no guarantee they will succeed. And even if they do, as Bärtl's study shows, popular YouTubers often work for minimum wage—or less.

Those who fail might find themselves unemployed with an unexplainable gap in their résumé. Some try to avoid this by keeping their job while using their free time to create videos. But this too can be detrimental to the poster's career. Most employers do not want to attract controversy. They might have a problem with an employee who is in the spotlight, voicing divisive opinions or promoting outside brands on social media.

Whatever a person's employment status, anyone hoping to become a social media star is giving up his or her precious personal privacy. Sharing every thought online with a large number of strangers can have unintended negative consequences. "It can . . . be downright dangerous," writes digital marketer and content creator Amy Baker. "Many YouTubers face questions

Wannabe Kidfluencer

Ryan Kaji is often called a kidfluencer, a kid who influences the toy-buying decisions of his 24 million subscribers. Kaji was eight years old in 2019 when he earned $26 million reviewing toys on his Ryan's World YouTube channel. Kaji receives hundreds of free toys in the mail every month, and his videos have generated over 30 billion views.

The success of Ryan's World inspired a number of wannabe kidfluencers, who have found that YouTube success is not as easy as Kaji makes it seem. In 2016 a Dallas seven-year-old named Dane posted a video called *1 Subs Yas* thanking his grandmother for being the first subscriber (sub) to his channel. The video went viral on YouTube, and Dane quickly gained nineteen thousand subscribers. In 2018 Dane was mentioned by social media superstar PewDiePie. Dane's channel quickly attracted three hundred thousand subscribers, earning him around $9,000. But Dane was unable to keep up with the demands of maintaining a popular channel. He began losing thousands of subscribers, and his last video, posted in 2019, was called *My Channel Is Pretty Much Dying*. Dane said he felt pressure to make more videos, but he was too sad to do so.

Dane's channel still had 394,000 subscribers in 2020, but his story shows that most kids are not prepared for the type of stress experienced by social media creators. Nor are they ready for the disappointment associated with failure. But as long as kidfluencers rule social media platforms, thousands will continue to try to follow in Kaji's footsteps.

about their love life, their family, their friends, their mistakes, and other invasive questions, even when their channel is not a lifestyle vlog or personality-driven. YouTubers are often stopped in the street, or more troubling: followed, stalked or harassed in their home."[26]

Burning Out

Even those who possess the creativity, camera presence, and communication skills to reach the top find that social media success does not always equal happiness. Actor and comedian Olga Kay understands this only too well. Kay began posting content before anyone was making a living on social media. She was a professional circus juggler in Russia before moving to Los Angeles in 2007 at age twenty-five. A friend suggested she upload videos of her live juggling performances to YouTube. She was so unfamiliar with the platform that she initially thought it was called U2.com and wondered why the Irish rock band U2 hosted a video-sharing channel. But Kay quickly came to understand the concept. Rather than posting juggling videos, she created comical stories for a show called *Emo Girl*, which featured her as an autobiographical character named Razor Blade who hated everything. Kay also played a second character, a happy person who was emo girl's roommate. As Kay says, "One character was positive, one was negative. I think a lot of young girls could relate to that."[27]

"Many YouTubers face questions about their love life, their family, their friends, their mistakes, and other invasive questions, even when their channel is not a lifestyle vlog or personality-driven."[26]

—Amy Baker, content creator

Kay put her life on hold to spend her days writing, filming, editing, and posting stories. By 2014 she had over 1 million subscribers and was making twenty-three videos a week. Kay was also willing to take advantage of every opportunity; she developed a fashion and beauty channel (three videos a week) and a comedy gaming channel (fourteen videos a week). Like others who

At the height of her popularity, social media star Olga Kay (pictured) had 1 million subscribers, but the demands of making twenty-three videos each week left her feeling burned out.

achieve this level of social media success, Kay was able to earn a living from her fame by attracting brand partnerships and selling her own line of merchandise. However, Kay says the effort became too much to bear. "I covered all the bases and all the genres on YouTube, but I was making so many videos that I was burned out," she explains. "I realized that to continue to be successful on

YouTube I had to keep pumping out content. I felt like my creativity was slipping away. . . . I didn't want to be someone who has to wake up every morning and put makeup on to go in front of the camera."[28] Kay stopped posting content in 2016, and her audience quickly found others to follow.

Algorithmic Uncertainties

Many popular YouTubers are young adults with little job experience or understanding of the business world. But their success requires them to sign merchandise deals, manage support staff, and remain relevant in a highly competitive market. Perhaps the most difficult part of the job is trying to understand YouTube Analytics, the complex numerical data concerning views, likes, watch times, comments, shares, and engagement rates (the number of people who interact with the content).

While these numbers might make a creator's eyes glaze over, YouTube Analytics powers the algorithms that determine whether a channel lives or dies. Researcher Zoe Glatt explains:

> YouTube's algorithms prefer channels that have regular uploads and a narrow focus in terms of content. . . . Creators are encouraged to pursue a quantity-over-quality approach if they want to achieve success on YouTube. This, combined with a lack of clarity about what content exactly YouTube will promote and what might be demonetized, leads to an extremely precarious and stressful working life for creators.

YouTube is notoriously secretive about how its algorithms work. Glatt refers to this as algorithmic uncertainty. This phenomenon causes creators to limit their creativity to stay within what they assume are the expectations of the algorithm. Many burn out from worrying if the algorithm will favor their newest content.

Quoted in Chris Stokel-Walker, "Why YouTubers Are Feeling the Burn," *Guardian* (Manchester, UK), August 12, 2018. www.theguardian.com.

At the Mercy of Algorithms

Kay used her YouTube money to start a successful fashion line, but the negative aspects of her experience are common among social media superstars. YouTubers, TikTokers, and other influencers are expected to post videos on a weekly schedule. And viewers expect every video to be engaging. This can create a great deal of anxiety, according to game reviewer Matt Lees: "It's not enough to simply create great things. The audience expect consistency. They expect frequency."[29] And while Lees and other YouTubers do not work for a boss, they are at the mercy of artificial intelligence algorithms that decide whether they succeed or fail.

When someone posts a video that receives millions of views, algorithms take note of the traffic and recommend the poster's other videos. This earns the poster's channel additional viewers, subscribers, and advertisers, which translates into more money. While most YouTubers are initially excited by their rising numbers, the demand can be overwhelming. In Lees's case he was working twenty hours a day, fearful that missing even a single upload would lower his numbers. "It's incredibly easy to slip off the radar and lose favor with the algorithm that gave you your wings,"[30] Lees concludes.

Lees says he was on a video-production treadmill, unable to sleep or even rest. The exhaustion showed in his videos, which became overly critical and harsh in tone. Ironically, the divisive content increased his viewership, another result of algorithms. Numerous studies have shown that people spend more time on social media sites when they are presented with controversial content that makes them feel angry, excited, or aggrieved. Companies like YouTube and Facebook make money off this basic aspect of human nature; the longer a user is engaged with a site—for whatever reason—the more advertisements they will see. As Lees remarks, "Divisive content is the king of online media today, and YouTube heavily boosts anything that riles people up. It's one of the most toxic things: the point at which you're breaking down is the point at which the algorithm loves you the most."[31]

The job of social media star requires more than the constant production of quality content. A large percentage of posters are self-employed entrepreneurs who have to personally deal with the numerous business aspects associated with running a popular channel. They have to keep records, pay taxes, and promote themselves on other social media sites. Posters also need to react to the constant stream of user comments and emails, which can be insulting and even threatening. People online are prone to misinterpreting comments and taking offense at minor slights. Amy Baker writes, "It is impossible to always be 100% clear about everything you say so that every single viewer understands your perspective. There will be times where your words, your tone, or your looks will be interpreted in a way you never intended, and you need to be accepting of the fact that this will always happen, no matter how much you try to explain."[32]

Lees was overwhelmed by the continuous stream of user comments soliciting his advice or offering criticism of his videos. He developed health problems while his mental well-being suffered. Lees says what started out as the greatest job in the world left him feeling lonely and depressed.

Social media stars find little sympathy from fans who expect their idols to present a happy face to the world. Fans who work at regular jobs or attend school find it difficult to imagine how someone like Tyler Blevins can complain. Blevins, known as Ninja, is the most-followed gamer on the video livestreaming service Twitch. He makes $500,000 every month live broadcasting himself playing *Fortnite*. Much of his money comes from fans who donate small amounts on Patreon, hoping that Ninja will thank them on the air. But as Ninja wrote on Twitter in 2018, "Wanna

> "The point at which you're breaking down is the point at which the algorithm loves you the most."[31]
>
> —Matt Lees, game reviewer

Tyler Blevins (pictured), also known as Ninja, earns $500,000 every month live broadcasting himself playing Fortnite.

know the struggles of streaming over other jobs? . . . I left for less than 48 hours and lost 40,000 subscribers on Twitch. I'll be back today . . . grinding again."[33]

Reaching the Breaking Point

Kati Morton understands how being a popular creator can take a toll on a person. She is a mental health expert who began posting YouTube videos about eating disorders, anxiety, and other issues in 2011. But Morton's own mental health began to suffer as she forced herself to upload five videos each week while also maintaining a private practice as a therapist. She became exhausted, irritable, and sad. In 2018 Morton took a one-month break to give herself time to recover.

Most social media influencers are not trained to recognize symptoms of job burnout. Some push themselves beyond their abilities and suffer as a result. Nothing better exemplifies the dark side of the influencer economy than the 2019 suicide of twenty-nine-year-old YouTuber Etika. Daniel Desmond "Etika" Amofah specialized in Nintendo gaming videos, particularly the fighting game franchise *Super Smash Bros.* His over-the-top reactions—including screams and falling back into his chair—helped attract 1.3 million followers to his various YouTube channels and spawned several memes. But Etika had mental health issues that were aggravated by his intense upload schedule and the pressure related to life as a public persona.

Etika was a model and rapper in Brooklyn, New York, when he began broadcasting his reaction to gaming streams on YouTube in 2012. Fans became concerned about Etika in October 2018 when he uploaded pornography to his main YouTube channel, a deliberate violation of the platform's policies. After YouTube deleted the channel, Etika posted an erratic video to Reddit in which he expressed suicidal thoughts. A few hours later he posted a message on Reddit claiming to be fine. He said he had been overdramatic and signed off with an LOL.

But Etika was not fine, and his mental health continued to deteriorate in a very public manner. In April 2019 he posted anti-Semitic comments, referred to himself as God, and blocked many of his close friends from his accounts. After he posted a video of himself holding a gun, police were called to his apartment. Etika livestreamed the thirty-minute standoff on Instagram. "A lot of people think they can troll and abuse online personalities, forgetting they're not immune to mental health problems," Etika said during the event. "Because they're perceived as able to make a living online, they're not allowed to have social or mental problems."[34] He was detained by police after the event and ended up briefly in a mental hospital.

While many of Etika's followers were concerned about his behavior, some took joy in tormenting him. People made mocking memes, posted jokes about mental illness, and spammed Etika's Twitter account with clown emojis. Ex-girlfriend Alice Pika says Etika obsessed over the harmful posts, and this type of negative reinforcement increased his feelings of isolation and despair. In June 2019 Etika posted his final video to YouTube with these words: "[Being a social media star] can give you an image of what you want your life to be and it can get blown completely out of proportion, dog. Unfortunately, it consumed me."[35] Hours later, Etika drowned himself in the East River.

Alan Bunney is a physician and former professional gamer who founded the e-sports brand Panda Global. Bunney, who works with prominent Twitch streamers, was saddened when he heard about Etika's struggles. Bunney offered this advice to social media consumers:

> If you see someone tweet that they're in a bad place—do you know how hard it is for them to say? They craft this public persona, and for them to break that image and say, "I'm not okay," that's [a] hard, bad place. People need to immediately realize this is not a joke. They need to say, "We will support you, we will continue to consume your content when you are better. You can take a month away, and I will come back and watch your videos. I'll still be there for you no matter what happens." It's so important we say that.[36]

Intolerable Egomaniacs

Etika's story illustrates that influencers are just like everyone else. And the drive to remain relevant on a constantly changing medium can push some people over the edge. In 2019 Danish influencer Fie Laursen posted a suicide note on her Instagram feed, which had over 350,000 followers. Laursen's family intervened and prevented a tragedy, but the note remained up for two days, attracting thirty thousand likes.

While influencer depression and other mental issues attract the most attention in the media, there is another aspect to social media stardom that is also damaging to individuals. Social media stars often become intolerable egomaniacs. As self-described Instafamous star Verity Johnson puts it, "I became convinced that I was *so* fascinating. If I was the center of attention on my phone, that should translate into being the center of attention in real life. It makes you the worst kind of [jerk]: entitled, self-obsessed, and incredibly dull because the only thing you think about is yourself."[37]

Johnson says her hot photos attracted advertisers who sent her everything from free lingerie to cell phones and protein powder. But she found herself trapped in a mind-numbing schedule, forced to produce a steady stream of glamour shots alone, without the help of makeup artists and professional photographers. Rather than having fun, she had to manufacture moments that looked exciting to her followers. As Johnson explains:

> "Instafame fed my own vanity and insecurity until it became almost impossible to control them and make space for my better self."[38]
>
> —Verity Johnson, Instagram influencer

Social media feeds those darkest parts of every personality, encouraging you to rant on Twitter, brag on Facebook, or be vain on Insta. Vanity sells on the 'Gram. The hotter the pic, the better it does, so the more time you spend in the mirror creating them. Staying Instafamous relies on you mining the depths of your own narcissism. . . . Instafame fed my own vanity and insecurity until it became almost impossible to control them and make space for my better self.[38]

Johnson worried continually that her fame would slip away, something that made her even more desperate to hold on to it. But she stopped posting to Instagram in 2019 and now considers herself an ex-influencer. "I realized in order to stay Instafamous I'd have had to nurture the most pathetic parts of my own psyche," she states. "And honestly, no amount of free ombre activewear is worth that."[39]

More Money, More Problems

In 2019 the ten most popular YouTube creators earned a combined $162 million. But for every Instafamous YouTuber, there were thousands of imitators trying to cash in on the person's success. A few strivers possess the drive, talent, and camera-friendly presence necessary to attract a widespread following. The greater majority struggle with scarce subscribers, a lack of likes, and a dismal number of views. And while the floundering wannabes dream of social media success, those at the top, whose names are known to millions, have their own unique problems.

Chapter Four

Profiting from Bad Advice

Almost everyone knows that social media is filled with bad advice, irrational conspiracy theories, and outright lies. Despite this common knowledge, some social media influencers profit by promoting dangerous practices and sketchy products. One of those influencers had over 142,000 followers on YouTube in 2020. Cole Robinson is not a gamer, fashion vlogger, or comedian. He calls himself a fasting coach. Robinson promotes dry fasting—he tells people to not drink water for up to seven days. Robinson also endorses hard dry fasting, which means also giving up showering, hand washing, and even tooth brushing. Robinson has no medical degree or training in nutrition or biology. But he has produced more than a dozen videos telling his followers that if they stop drinking water, they will lose weight, overcome depression, slow aging, and cure herpes, stomach flu, and other health problems.

Medical experts warn that depriving the body of water will cause internal organs to fail, resulting in death within three days. Robinson, who films himself dry fasting, exhibits common symptoms of water deprivation, including sleeplessness, severe muscle cramps, stomach aches, nausea, and headaches. But the obvious health risks associated with water deprivation have not slowed the number of people who recommend dry fasting on social media sites. Physician assistant Louise Cardellina asserts, "I thought [dry fasting] was a joke, then when I heard it was a reality, I was alarmed. It's not based in any logic or science and anyone who is touting this is doing you a disservice."[40] Still, Robinson has thousands of followers who dry fast for several days at a time under the mistaken belief that the body pulls water from damaged or weak cells to hydrate the healthy ones.

> "The majority of the blogs could not be considered credible sources of weight management information, as they often presented opinion as fact and failed to meet . . . nutritional criteria."[41]
>
> —Christina Sabbagh, nutrition researcher

Bad diet advice knows no national boundaries. In 2019 a team of researchers at the University of Glasgow studied weight management claims made by some of the most popular influencers in the United Kingdom (UK). The researchers found that only one out of nine leading bloggers could be trusted. Lead researcher Christina Sabbagh explains, "We found that the majority of the blogs could not be considered credible sources of weight management information, as they often presented opinion as fact and failed to meet UK nutritional criteria. This is potentially harmful, as these blogs reach such a wide audience."[41]

Diet Disasters

In addition to offering dangerous advice, some social media influencers promote sponsored weight-loss products such as diet shakes, detox teas, and appetite suppressant lollipops. Most of these products do not work as advertised, and some have side effects that are often ignored by influencers. This is particularly true of diet and detox teas that have names like FitTea, Skinny Me Tea, and Bootea. These teas are promoted by the Kardashian-Jenner family, Cardi B, and others. Influencers can make a lot of money for their promotions. In 2016 athlete and YouTuber Arianna Dantone said that a company that sells herbal diet tea offered her nearly $12,000 plus $5 for each new customer and 5 percent of sales that came through her account.

Dantone turned down the offer because she understands that diet teas and detox teas are unhealthy. The main ingredient in most of these teas is an herb known as senna, an extremely powerful laxative. Senna is used by doctors to treat constipation and to clear the intestines before colonoscopy diagnostic tests. Senna causes temporary water weight loss by sending users to the bathroom more often. While Kim Kardashian looks beautiful and perfectly composed when posing with a package of diet tea on Instagram, those who ingest senna experience stomach cramps, diarrhea, and the inability to control their bowel movements. Drinking diet teas on a regular basis is extremely unhealthy. The body does not properly absorb nutrients and calories from food. And senna can cause the intestines to become dependent on it. A person who is dependent on senna and stops using it

Some social media influencers promote products, such as detox teas, that either do not work as advertised or have undesirable side effects.

can experience constipation, bloating, and ironically, weight gain. Additionally, the teas have been blamed for unplanned pregnancies; the laxative effect prevents the proper absorption of birth control pills.

Jamil Fights Back

People who struggle to lose weight are vulnerable to social media stars who promise instant results. But one celebrity has made it her personal mission to regulate the promotion of diet products on social media. Jameela Jamil starred on the hit TV series *The Good Place* from 2016 to 2020. Jamil has frequently criticized celebrity influencers for promoting bogus diet products that have no scientific basis for their claims. She says influencers set impossible beauty standards by posting photos that are filtered and Photoshopped to make the subjects appear flawless.

Jamil, who calls herself a former teenage anorexic, explains the harm caused by the diet industry working in tandem with celebrity influencers:

> "In my day, you'd have to search for ages to find this toxic [diet] information, but now it finds you because of algorithms that know your age, sex and what you're into."[42]
>
> —Jameela Jamil, actor

In my day, you'd have to search for ages to find this toxic [diet] information, but now it finds you because of algorithms that know your age, sex and what you're into. Therefore it's the worst it's ever been. Teenage suicides, eating disorder rates, the amount having cosmetic surgery and committing self-harm—they are all at the highest they've ever been. There's no way this isn't a correlation with what they're being exposed to online.[42]

Jamil says she mutes, blocks, or deletes anyone who promotes diet products or who makes her feel bad about the way she looks or the way she lives. And Jamil felt so strongly about

Television celebrity Jameela Jamil frequently criticizes social media influencers who promote bogus diet products.

the issue that she launched a petition in 2019 on Change.org. Over 244,000 people signed the petition called "Stop Celebrities Promoting Toxic Diet Products on Social Media." The petition was sent to Twitter, Facebook, Snapchat, and Instagram. One social media site took notice. In 2019 Instagram instituted a rule that said if a post promotes a weight loss product or cosmetic procedure, users younger than eighteen will be prohibited from seeing the post. Instagram also banned any content that makes a miraculous claim about a diet or weigh loss product. Posts that make such claims will be removed.

Cosmetic Catastrophes

Jamil uses her celebrity to warn young women about the dangers of fad diets and cosmetic surgery. But other popular influencers with no medical training earn money promoting risky procedures and dangerous devices. In 2018 social media star Erin Ziering had over 282,000 Instagram followers. Ziering, wife of *Beverly Hills, 90210* star Ian Ziering, posted an endorsement for Biocell breast implants, made by the pharmaceutical company Allergan. Ziering, who was dressed in a pink tutu against a pink backdrop while promoting the product, did not disclose the general health risks associated with breast implants. Additionally, she posted the vlog several months after the US Food and Drug Administration (FDA) issued a warning that women who used the Biocell implants risked developing a type of cancer called breast implant–associated anaplastic large cell lymphoma. Ironically, Ziering dedicated her post to breast cancer survivors.

Ziering also promotes Botox, a drug made from botulinum toxin. Botox reduces wrinkles in the forehead and around the eyes by causing paralysis of facial muscles. Other social media influencers promote lip implants. According to the American Society of Plastic Surgeons, there is a lip implant procedure done about every nineteen minutes, an increase of 48 percent since 2000. And the clients seeking cosmetic procedures are younger than ever. Journalist Suzanne Zuppello claims that the increase is due to teens and young adults who are inundated with celebrity images at a time when they are struggling to fit in. Zuppello insists:

> Instagram ads . . . are selling not just a product but an entire lifestyle. Rather than buying a single-page ad or a minute-long TV or radio spot, companies benefit from the candor and storytelling on influencers' feeds. However, selling a pair of shoes or luggage as part of a lifestyle is far different from selling pharmaceuticals, medical devices, and other health-related products.[43]

Promoting Eating Disorders

Never before in history have so many people been exposed to such a wide variety of diets and fitness trends. Thanks to social media stars and celebrity influencers, consumers can learn about paleo diets, detoxing, infrared saunas, and extreme cycling workouts. Even seemingly harmless diets, like clean eating, can cause problems.

The clean eating philosophy involves eating only unprocessed organic foods, preferably those that are locally grown. But according to nutritionist Jaclyn London, "What was once a sense of awareness about food seems to have spiraled into . . . yet another form of body and food-shaming [on social media]." London says that some who promote clean eating discredit those who consume nonapproved "dirty foods." This has led to the growth of a previously little-known eating disorder called orthorexia nervosa.

People with orthorexia nervosa become obsessed with health, wellness, and clean eating. They avoid prepared foods and dishes for which they cannot assess the ingredients. The disorder is similar to anorexia nervosa, which is an obsession with body image and weight loss. Both disorders focus on food restriction, which can lead to lowered metabolism, loss of menstruation, brittle hair, dry skin, bone loss, and other issues.

Over 30 million Americans suffer from eating disorders. Experts say social media influencers who rave about the latest diet fads, while posting Photoshopped pictures that make them look very thin, are adding to the problem. Social media users are bombarded by messages concerning diet, weight, and health. They need to realize that influencers and celebrities are not nutritionists, and their advice is not necessarily scientifically sound.

Quoted in Ellie Krieger, "There's No Such Thing as 'Bad Food.' Four Terms That Make Dietitians Cringe," *Washington Post*, June 5, 2019. www.washingtonpost.com.

Government Guidelines

While it seems like advertisers can say or do whatever they want on social media, they are regulated by two government agencies. The FDA tests and controls production of prescription drugs, medical devices, and other health-related products. The Federal

Trade Commission (FTC) protects consumers from false advertising and other forms of fraud and has strict guidelines that regulate what companies can say in commercials on television, on radio, and in print. The FDA and FTC work together to regulate the claims of pharmaceutical makers, which is why a narrator can be heard rapidly describing the side effects of a prescription drug at the end of a TV commercial for such a product.

The truth-in-advertising regulations issued by the FDA and FTC also apply to anyone promoting products on the internet, whether it is on a website or a social media site. But the regulations are written in complicated legal jargon. While it is up to each social media influencer to read and understand the guidelines, most do not. According to a 2017 study from the influencer ad agency Mediakix, only 7 percent of sponsored content posted by the top fifty Instagram influencers adhered to FTC guidelines and regulations. The A-list celebrity influencers who did not meet the requirements included Selena Gomez, Beyoncé, PewDiePie, and others, with a combined following of 2.5 billion. The study found that the Kardashian-Jenner family alone had at least one hundred Instagram endorsements that violated FTC rules. The reality TV stars failed to inform viewers that they were paid for product endorsements by companies such as Puma, Calvin Klein, and FitTea. Bonnie Patten, executive director of the consumer group Truth in Advertising, explains, "When it comes to sponsored social media posts, the law is clear—unless it's self-evident that an Instagram post is an advertisement, a clear and prominent disclosure is required so that consumers understand that what they are viewing is an ad."[44]

"When it comes to sponsored social media posts, the law is clear—unless it's self-evident that an Instagram post is an advertisement, a clear and prominent disclosure is required so that consumers understand that what they are viewing is an ad."[44]

—Bonnie Patten, consumer advocate

In 2017 the FTC sent warning letters to over ninety celebrities—and the brands that sponsored them—asking what steps were being taken to disclose sponsored posts on Instagram. Some who received the letters changed their practices to alert viewers that they are being paid to promote products. Others ignored the FTC and continued to practice business as usual because they understood that government regulators do not have the money or the staff required to monitor the 5 million sponsored posts that appear annually on Instagram.

> "There can be a lot of false health claims out there, so it's important to ask where that information or advice is coming from."[45]
>
> —Mark Hyman, physician

The FTC often relies on consumers to report advertising violations. But few consumers understand FTC rules, and fewer still are motivated to contact a government agency when watching their favorite social media celebrities push products. Influencers benefit from the fact that consumers are not taking steps to protect themselves. A 2019 study by the Cleveland Clinic found that 44 percent of Americans have taken diet, health, and fitness advice from social media influencers on Facebook, Instagram, YouTube, and other sites. This is risky says Dr. Mark Hyman of the Cleveland Clinic, "There can be a lot of false health claims out there, so it's important to ask where that information or advice is coming from."[45]

Medical Misinformation

Perhaps the most widespread bad medical advice on social media comes from people called anti-vaxxers. The anti-vaxxer movement is built on the false belief that childhood vaccinations against measles, mumps, and other preventable diseases cause autism and other medical problems. In reality, vaccinations prevent more than 21 million illnesses and 732,000 deaths among children in the United States alone, according to the Centers for Disease Control and Prevention.

Unvaccinated children are vulnerable to deadly diseases. They also pose a risk to other people, who could potentially contract these diseases. This could lead to an epidemic. Factual information could prevent this but social media algorithms often

Perhaps the most widespread bad medical advice on social media comes from people called anti-vaxxers, who promote the false belief that childhood vaccinations cause autism and other medical problems.

guide people to sites that contain misinformation about vaccines. A 2019 study by the *Guardian* news outlet found that Google searches for the term "vaccine" often sent users to anti-vax videos and Facebook groups. (Facebook does not allow anti-vax advertisements but does not censor anti-vax groups.) YouTube claims it tries to monitor videos that misinform users in harmful ways. But the anti-vax message is widespread. According to a study by the Royal Society for Public Health in the UK, half of all parents with small children have been exposed to anti-vax misinformation on social media. While some call for social media platforms to censor anti-vaxxers, it can be an impossible job. Some of the anti-vax posts with the most likes and shares have been traced to trolls working for foreign governments that are deliberately trying to create conflict and destabilize society.

Anti-Vax Bots and Trolls

In 2018 researchers at George Washington University examined thousands of anti-vax tweets sent from 2014 to 2017. Three-quarters of the tweets made unscientific statements meant to spread the false message that vaccines were unsafe. The study's name reveals what was found: "Weaponized Health Communication: Twitter Bots and Russian Trolls Amplify the Vaccine Debate." The study's lead author, David Broniatowski, explains the significance of the findings:

> The vast majority of Americans believe vaccines are safe and effective, but looking at Twitter gives the impression that there is a lot of debate. It turns out that many anti-vaccine tweets come from accounts whose provenance is unclear. These might be bots, human users or "cyborgs"—hacked accounts that are sometimes taken over by bots. Although it's impossible to know exactly how many tweets were generated by bots and trolls, our findings suggest that a significant portion of the online discourse about vaccines may be generated by malicious actors with a range of hidden agendas.

> The agendas of the trolls and bots include spreading false information and promoting discord to intentionally harm society. There were similar widespread attacks from those known as content polluters during the 2016 presidential election.

Quoted in GW Today, "Russian Trolls, Bots Influence Vaccine Discussion on Twitter," August 24, 2018. https://gwtoday.gwu.edu.

Dangerous Stunts, Stupid Challenges

Whatever the motivations of anti-vaxxers, there are plenty of popular influencers who amplify dangerous behavior simply to attract eyeballs. And one of the stunts performed by prankster Ryan Hamilton, or Hammy, caused permanent damage to at least one innocent bystander. Hammy is YouTube famous; in 2020 his Hammy TV channel had nearly half a million subscribers. Hammy often shoots low-budget comical videos with his girlfriend. While Hammy's stunts can be entertaining and amusing, they can be hazardous when attempted by his fans. In 2018 a woman named Laurie Redmond said one of Hammy's prank videos ruined the life of her thirteen-year-old daughter, Cindy. The video, called *How to Get Your Girlfriend to Put Her Phone Down*, had an astounding 246 million views, according to Redmond. The video shows Hammy's girlfriend talking on the phone in various scenarios such as exercising, shopping, and sitting on the couch. Hammy sneaks up behind her each time and blasts her with an air horn.

The video was obviously practiced with Hammy's girlfriend to make her shocked reactions seem hilarious. However, when Cindy was on the phone at a friend's house, the friend's stepfather tried to imitate Hammy's stunt, and the outcome was not funny. Laurie picks up the story: "My teenage daughter was blasted with an air horn to get her to put her phone down. She is now in pain every second of every day. . . . Cindy has burning pain in her ears all the time. With all noise louder than ordinary conversation, she feels like she is being stabbed in the ear. Her ears ring."[10] Air powered horns like those used at football games are so loud that they can cause hyperacusis—noise induced pain—and permanent hearing loss.

Hammy is not the only so-called prankster to blast people with painfully loud noises. Jake Paul, brother of YouTuber Logan Paul, shot a video while driving around Los Angeles in a car equipped with a super-loud train horn. Paul filmed the faces of frightened pedestrians as he blared the horn at them as they crossed in front of his car. Most stunts are not illegal, and there is no law that can hold stunt performers responsible for their actions. But one man sued Paul for negligence, emotional distress, and battery after his hearing was damaged. (The outcome of the lawsuit remains unknown.)

Logan Paul is also famous for promoting controversial pranks. In 2020 Paul's YouTube channel, Logan Paul Vlogs, had over 20 million subscribers and 4.8 billion views. Paul appeals to his audience made up mostly of teenage boys by using crass humor and performing cruel stunts such as Tasering a rat. Paul was widely criticized in 2018 when he tweeted that he would eat one Tide laundry detergent pod for every retweet of a joke he posted. Paul was referencing the viral internet trend called the Tide Pod Challenge, which encouraged participants to eat laundry soap.

The Tide Pod Challenge began in 2017 when an estimated hundred teenagers filmed themselves intentionally eating poisonous Tide pods. This stunt can cause vomiting, breathing difficulties, loss of consciousness, and even death. Paul did not initiate the challenge, which caused several kids to be hospitalized with serious injuries, but he was criticized for promoting it. As journalist Josh Katzowitz writes, "Tide Pods have become meme-worthy, and with some YouTubers chomping down on the laundry detergent packets in order to increase their viewership—and considering how young Paul's fanbase is—his tweet is an irresponsible one."[47]

The Tide Pod Challenge is just one of many stupid stunts that have gained traction on social media. TikTok encourages users to post challenges, and its algorithms reward those who come up with dares that go viral. This has led to stunts in which people set themselves on fire, choke their friends to unconsciousness, and eat extremely hot ghost peppers. While those who post dumb deeds might not be influencers, some are hoping to become internet famous by driving viewers to their videos.

Let the Buyer Beware

People have imitated commercial fads and fashions for decades. Today the average American spends two and a half hours each day on social media, so it should come as no surprise that many take advice from YouTubers and the Instafamous. But sellers have been fooling buyers for so long that there is a Latin phrase that has become an English proverb. *Caveat emptor* means "Let the buyer beware." It is short for *Caveat emptor, quia ignorare non debuit quod jus alienum emit*, or "Let a purchaser beware, for he ought not to be ignorant of the nature of the property which he is buying from another party."

The oldest known use of caveat emptor can be traced to 1523, providing historical evidence that people have been getting swindled for centuries. But like almost everything else about the internet, the bilking is happening faster and in greater numbers than ever before.

While people tend to trust mommy bloggers and celebrities who seem to have their best interest in mind, social media influence is mainly about money. If promoting a product on social media was suddenly made illegal, the number of influencers would dwindle. But as it stands today, the risk that an influencer will be caught and fined for violating medical or advertising guidelines is practically zero. So social media devotees need to be extremely skeptical. The words that renowned writer Edgar Allan Poe wrote in 1845 remain relevant today: "Believe nothing you hear, and only half of that you see."[48]

Source Notes

Introduction: The New Entertainment

1. Julia Alexander, "TikTok Took Over VidCon, and YouTube Is Next," *The Verge*, July 15, 2019. www.theverge.com.
2. Quoted in Paige Leskin, "American Kids Want to Be Famous on YouTube, and Kids in China Want to Go to Space: Survey," *Business Insider*, July 17, 2019. www.businessinsider.com.
3. Kevin Roose, "Don't Scoff at Influencers. They're Taking Over the World," *New York Times*, July 16, 2019. www.nytimes.com.

Chapter One: Billions of Hits, Millions of Dollars

4. Quoted in Chavie Lieber, "How and Why Do Influencers Make So Much Money? The Head of an Influencer Agency Explains," *Vox*, November 28, 2018. www.vox.com.
5. Vicenzo Tsai, "Why Do People Watch PewDiePie on YouTube?," *Quora*, September 3, 2016. www.quora.com.
6. Quoted in BBC, "Evan Edinger: The Five Ways YouTubers Make Money," December 17, 2017. www.bbc.co.uk.
7. Georgia Bynum, "Tik Tok Takeover," *Yale Daily News*, February 6, 2020. https://yaledailynews.com.
8. Ken Scrudato, "Musical.ly Star Baby Ariel's Fave Miami Hangs + Debut Single & Video 'Aww,'" *BlackBook*, December 1, 2017. https://bbook.com.
9. Quoted in Rebecca Jennings, "TikTok, Explained," *Vox*, July 12, 2019. www.vox.com.
10. Quoted in Dan Whateley, "A Crew of TikTok Stars Live Rent-Free in a Bel Air Mansion, but at Sway House You Have to Meet Your Content Quota," *Business Insider*, January 27, 2020. www.businessinsider.com.
11. Quoted in Whateley, "A Crew of TikTok Stars Live Rent-Free in a Bel Air Mansion, but at Sway House You Have to Meet Your Content Quota."

12. Bynum, "Tik Tok Takeover."

13. Quoted in Deanna Ting, "'Every Kid Wants to Be an Influencer': Why TikTok Is Taking Off with Gen Z," Digiday, February 7, 2020. https://digiday.com.

Chapter Two: Mainstream Social Media Superstars

14. Quoted in Chuck Dauphin, "Kane Brown Talks Going Platinum and Buying His Mother a Car for Her Birthday," *Billboard*, November 16, 2017. www.billboard.com.

15. Quoted in Shan Li, "Emily Schuman Whipped Up Cupcakes and Cashmere in Her Spare Time," *Los Angeles Times*, May 24, 2013. www.latimes.com.

16. Vivienne Decker, "From Blogging to E-Commerce, Emily Schuman of *Cupcakes and Cashmere* Expands Her Brand with New Site," *Forbes*, April 28, 2017. www.forbes.com.

17. Quoted in Decker, "From Blogging to E-Commerce, Emily Schuman of *Cupcakes and Cashmere* Expands Her Brand with New Site."

18. Quoted in Bob Morris, "Martha, Oprah . . . Gwyneth?," *New York Times*, February 21, 2009. www.nytimes.com.

19. Quoted in Joshua David Stein, "Gwyneth Paltrow's Goop Inspires Famous Imitators," *New York Times*, November 13, 2013. www.nytimes.com.

20. Quoted in Taffy Brodesser-Akner, "Gwyneth Paltrow's Company Worth $250 Million," *New York Times*, July 25, 2018. www.nytimes.com.

21. Liz Alton, "What You Can Learn from Goop's Social Media Strategy," Customer Contact Advisor, May 24, 2018. https://customercontactadvisor.blr.com.

22. Quoted in *Time*, "The 30 Most Influential Teens of 2015," October 27, 2015. https://time.com.

23. Quoted in Natalie Robehmed, "At 21, Kylie Jenner Becomes the Youngest Self-Made Billionaire Ever," *Forbes*, March 5, 2019. www.forbes.com.

24. Quoted in Rebecca Ungarino, "Kylie Jenner's Tweet That Whacked Snap's Stock Was One Year Ago—and Shares Have Never Really Recovered," Market Insider, February 21, 2019. https://markets.businessinsider.com.

Chapter Three: Reality Check

25. Quoted in Chris Stokel-Walker, "'Success' on YouTube Still Means a Life of Poverty," Bloomberg, February 26, 2018. www.bloomberg.com.

26. Amy Baker, "The Worst Things About Being a YouTuber," *Content Career* (blog), March 15, 2018. https://contentcareer.com.

27. Quoted in Chris Stokel-Walker, "YouTube at 15: What Happened to Some of the Platform's Biggest Early Stars," *The Guardian* (Manchester), February 16, 2020. www.theguardian.com.

28. Quoted in Stokel-Walker, "YouTube at 15."

29. Quoted in Simon Parkin, "The YouTube Stars Heading for Burnout: 'The Most Fun Job Imaginable Became Deeply Bleak,'" *The Guardian* (Manchester), September 8, 2018. www.theguardian.com.

30. Quoted in Parkin, "The YouTube Stars Heading for Burnout."

31. Quoted in Parkin, "The YouTube Stars Heading for Burnout."

32. Baker, "The Worst Things About Being a YouTuber."

33. Quoted in Parkin, "The YouTube Stars Heading for Burnout."

34. Quoted in Julia Alexander, "YouTuber Etika's Death Spurs Conversations About How Viewers React to Creators' Mental Health Struggles," The Verge, July 27, 2019. www.theverge.com.

35. Quoted in Alexander, "YouTuber Etika's Death Spurs Conversations About How Viewers React to Creators' Mental Health Struggles."

36. Quoted in Alexander, "YouTuber Etika's Death Spurs Conversations About How Viewers React to Creators' Mental Health Struggles."

37. Verity Johnson, "I Was Insta-Famous and It Was One of the Worst Things to Happen in My 20s," *The Guardian* (Manchester), July 18, 2019. www.theguardian.com.

38. Johnson, "I Was Insta-Famous and It Was One of the Worst Things to Happen in My 20s."

39. Johnson, "I Was Insta-Famous and It Was One of the Worst Things to Happen in My 20s."

Chapter Four: Profiting from Bad Advice

40. Quoted in Ryan Trowbridge, "Healthcare Providers Voice Concerns over 'Dry Fasting,'" Western Mass News, February 20, 2020. www.westernmassnews.com.

41. Quoted in Adam Forrest, "Social Media Influencers Are Dishing Out False Nutritional and Weight Loss Advice 90% of the Time," Business Insider, April 30, 2019. www.businessinsider.com.

42. Quoted in Olivia Blair and Katie O'Manney, "Jameela Jamil on Instagram's New Diet Products Policy: 'This Is an Issue at Its Peak,'" Elle, September 18, 2019. www.elle.com.

43. Suzanne Zuppello, "The Latest Instagram Influencer Frontier? Medical Promotions," Vox, February 15, 2019. www.vox.com.

44. Quoted in Rebecca Stewart, "Kardashian Family Accused of 'Deceptive' Marketing over Paid for Instagram Endorsements," The Drum, August 23, 2016. www.thedrum.com.

45. Quoted in Tracey Romero, "Almost Half of Americans Take Health, Wellness Advice from Social Media—but Should We?," Philly Voice, October 17, 2019. www.phillyvoice.com.

46. Laurie Redmond, "A YouTube-Inspired Prank Ruined My Daughter's Life," The Guardian (Manchester), April 17, 2018. www.theguardian.com.

47. Josh Katzowitz, "Logan Paul's Tide Pod Challenge Tweet Shows He Hasn't Changed," Daily Dot, February 5, 2018. www.dailydot.com.

48. Quoted in Mark Pesce, "Sadly, the Web Has Brought a Whole New Meaning to the Phrase 'Nothing Is True; Everything Is Permitted,'" The Register, March 5, 2020. www.theregister.co.uk.

For Further Research

Books

Tessa "Tezza" Barton, *InstaStyle: Curate Your Life, Create Stunning Photos, and Elevate Your Instagram Influence*. Indianapolis: Alpha, 2018.

Shane Birley, *The Vlogger's Handbook: Love It! Live It! Vlog It!* Irvine, CA: QEB, 2019.

Goali Saedi Bocci, *The Social Media Workbook for Teens: Skills to Help You Balance Screen Time, Manage Stress, and Take Charge of Your Life*. Oakland, CA: Instant Help, 2019.

Sean Cannell, *YouTube Secrets: The Ultimate Guide to Growing Your Following and Making Money as a Video Influencer*. Austin: Lioncrest, 2018.

Claire Edward, *Social Media and Mental Health: Handbook for Teens*. Newark, UK: Trigger, 2018.

Stuart Kallen, *Careers in Social Media*. San Diego, CA: ReferencePoint, 2020.

New York Times Editorial Staff, ed., *Social Media Influencers: Apps, Algorithms and Celebrities*. New York: New York Times Educational, 2019.

Chris Stokel-Walker, *YouTubers: How YouTube Shook Up TV and Created a New Generation of Stars*. Kingston upon Thames, UK: Canbury, 2019.

Internet Sources

Julia Alexander, "TikTok Took Over VidCon, and YouTube Is Next," The Verge, July 15, 2019. www.theverge.com.

Amy Baker, "The Worst Things About Being a YouTuber," *Content Career* (blog), March 15, 2018. https://contentcareer.com.

Olivia Blair and Katie O'Manney, "Jameela Jamil on Instagram's New Diet Products Policy: 'This Is an Issue at Its Peak,'" *Elle*, September 18, 2019. www.elle.com.

Chavie Lieber, "How and Why Do Influencers Make So Much Money? The Head of an Influencer Agency Explains," Vox, November 28, 2018. www.vox.com.

Taylor Lorenz, "Hype House and the Los Angeles TikTok Mansion Gold Rush," *New York Times*, January 3, 2020. www.nytimes.com.

Simon Parkin, "The YouTube Stars Heading for Burnout: 'The Most Fun Job Imaginable Became Deeply Bleak,'" *The Guardian* (Manchester), September 8, 2018. www.theguardian.com.

Natalie Robehmed, "At 21, Kylie Jenner Becomes the Youngest Self-Made Billionaire Ever," *Forbes*, March 5, 2019. www.forbes.com.

Websites

Facebook for Creators (www.facebook.com/creators). This Facebook how-to website for content creators focuses on getting started, shooting videos, writing blogs, and cross-posting with Instagram. The site provides tools for in-stream ads, monetizing content, and finding brand collaborations.

Famebit (www.famebit.com). This popular link-sharing platform, owned by Google/YouTube, pairs marketers with influencers. Prospective YouTubers can use the site to learn about marketing, paid sponsorships, and creating desirable content.

Influencer Marketing Association (https://influencermarketing association.org). This trade organization was founded to promote influencer industry guidelines, provide resources to marketing professionals, and educate the public. The association features blogs, hosts meetups, and publishes a newsletter.

Instagram Business (https://business.instagram.com). Instafamous wannabes can use this official Instagram website to learn everything they need to know about creating successful content, connecting with business, and targeting consumers. The site features blogs, success stories, and other relevant information.

TikTok Creator Marketplace (https://creatormarketplace.tiktok.com). This website provides a platform where ad agencies and brand promoters can connect with TikTok's top creators and influencers. Marketing directors can browse by keyword, country, and demographics and contact creators they wish to do business with.

Index

Picture Credits

Cover: Have a nice day Photo/Shutterstock

7: NYCStock/Shutterstock
11: JStone/Shutterstock
14: Kathy Hutchins/Shutterstock
20: Art_Photo/Shutterstock
26: David Leon Jr/Shutterstock
30: dennizn/Shutterstock
36: s_bukley/Shutterstock
39: pixinoo/Shutterstock
43: Featureflash Photo Agency/Shutterstock
47: lev radin/Shutterstock
54: Luna Vandoorne/Shutterstock
56: lev radin/Shutterstock
61: Africa Studio/Shutterstock

About the Author

Stuart A. Kallen is the author of more than 350 nonfiction books for children and young adults. He has written on topics ranging from the theory of relativity to the art of electronic dance music. In 2018 Kallen won a Green Earth Book Award from the Nature Generation environmental organization for his book *Trashing the Planet: Examining the Global Garbage Glut*. In his spare time he is a singer, songwriter, and guitarist in San Diego.